025 Grey

Information Technology

Kay Davies
and
Wendy Oldfield

Starting Science

Books in the series

Animals
Electricity and Magnetism
Floating and Sinking
Food
Hot and Cold
Information Technology
Light

Materials
The Senses
Skeletons and Movement
Sound and Music
Waste
Water
Weather

About this book

Information technology explores, at a simple level, the many ways in which we communicate with each other; from speech and signing to the latest advances in technology. Methods of sending messages are looked at, including telecommunications and satellite communications, together with storing and retrieving information on computer.

The activities are designed to strengthen each theme. They are all carefully measured to the abilities of younger children and so that they fall within their everyday experiences.

The main picture and its commentary may be taken as an introduction to the topic or as a focal point for further discussion. Each chapter can form a basis for extended topic work.

Teachers will find that in using this book, they are reinforcing the other core subjects of language and mathematics. Through its topic approach **Information Technology** covers aspects of the National Science Curriculum for key stage 1 (levels 1 to 3), for the following Attainment Targets: Exploration of science (AT 1), Types and uses of materials (AT 6), The scientific aspects of information technology including microelectronics (AT 12) and Sound and music (AT14).

First published in 1991 by
Wayland (Publishers) Ltd
61 Western Road, Hove
East Sussex, BN3 1JD, England

© Copyright 1991 Wayland (Publishers) Ltd

Typeset by DP Press Ltd, Sevenoaks, Kent
Printed in Italy by Rotolito Lombarda
 S.p.A., Milan
Bound in Belgium by Casterman S.A.

**British Library Cataloguing in
 Publication Data**
Davies, Kay 1946
1. Information. Communication & dissemination.
Effects of technological development
I. Title II. Oldfield, Wendy III. Series
025

ISBN 0 7502 0092 8

Editor: Cally Chambers

CONTENTS

Body talk	4
Getting the message	6
Write a letter	9
Give me a ring	11
Tuning in	13
TV time	14
Play it again	17
Moving moments	18
Giving orders	21
A good program	22
Print out	24
Safe in the bank	27
Satellites in space	29
Glossary	30
Finding out more	31
Index	32

All the words that first appear in **bold** in the text are explained in the glossary.

BODY TALK

When we are young, we learn to talk. We can ask for the things we want. We can pass on our news.

Sometimes we use only our bodies to talk to each other.

Try telling a friend these things without using any words: 'Meet me outside.' 'Get a glass of water.' 'Come and play football.' Think of some other things to tell them.

What do you think these people are saying?

It's   to

Answer: It is time to eat.

Some people cannot hear well.

They find it difficult to understand what is being said.

They use a special **sign language** to talk to their friends.

The clown can be very funny.
He makes us laugh but he doesn't have to say a word.

GETTING THE MESSAGE

Some machines that we use come from other countries.

They are made with picture signs on them.
This helps people all around the world to work them.
It doesn't matter that people speak different languages.

This television has no words on its controls. Instead, pictures tell you how to work it.

Can you see how to turn it ON and OFF, change channels, make it louder or brighter?

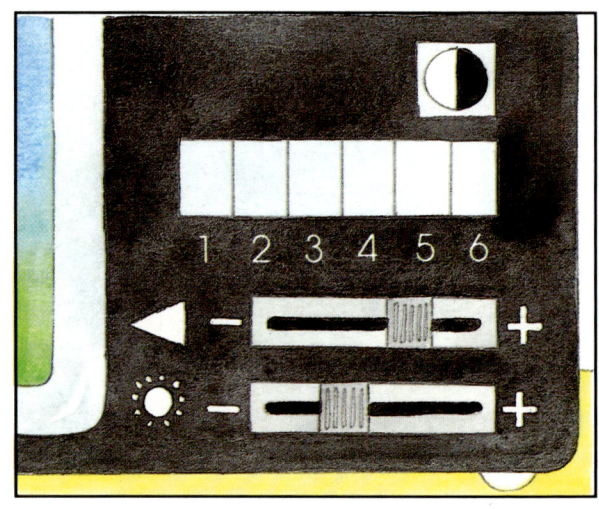

Airport   Danger/poison
No smoking   Telephone
Women/girls   Do not iron
Men/boys

Look at these signs.

Can you match them up with the meanings from the list?

Draw some picture signs of your own.

Can your friends understand them?

The safety sign is in different languages.
A quick look at the pictures tells us how to swim safely.

The letter-sorting machine can read the post-codes.
It makes sure your letter gets to the right town.

WRITE A LETTER

People learned to write letters thousands of years ago.

Their letters often took months to reach the right person.

Now a letter posted in your country can reach a friend in another country two days later, like this:

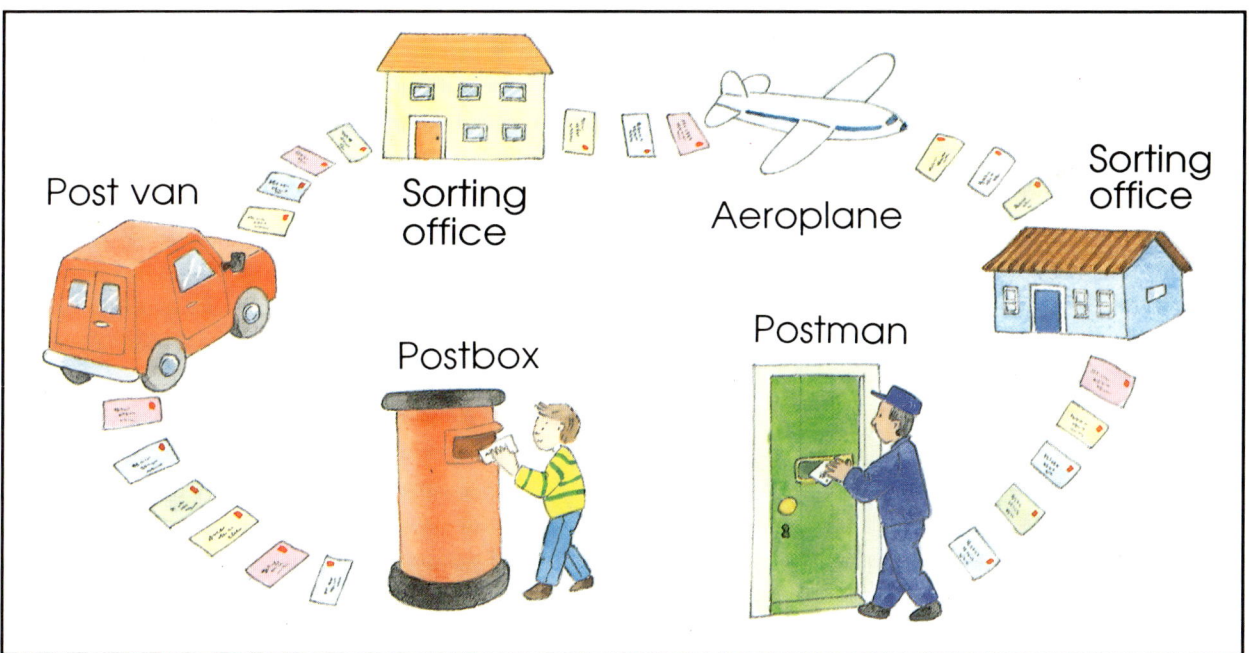

Groups of houses share the same post-code
This helps the post office to sort the letters quickly.

A post-code is written as part of an address. Can you write your address and post-code clearly?

Write a letter to a friend. Check that you have got their address and post-code right.

Lots of people make telephone calls at the same time.
How many people are using telephones in this picture?

GIVE ME A RING

The telephone changes your voice into electronic signals. These travel through wires to the telegraph pole.

The wires go underground to your local telephone exchange. The exchange can send the electronic signals to most parts of the world.

They can go under the sea through thin **optic fibres**. They can travel to **satellites** in space as invisible waves.

At the other end they come out sounding just like us.

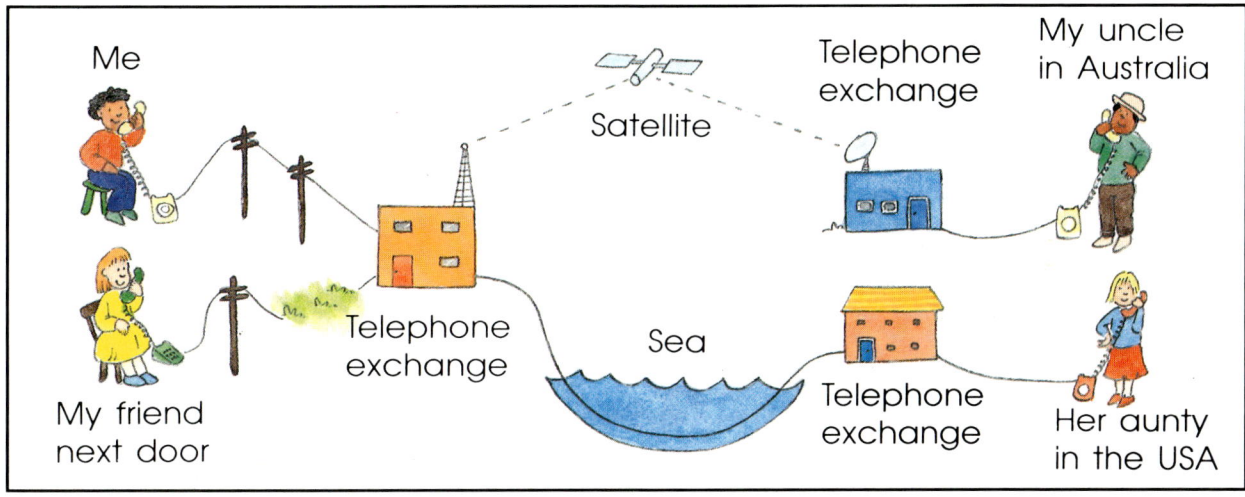

Fax machines send and receive messages and drawings through the telephone service.
The machine reads the piece of paper at one end.

It turns the message into electronic signals and sends it to another machine. An exact copy is printed out.

The helicopter has been sent a radio message.
It has flown to rescue someone who is in danger.

TUNING IN

Some broadcasting stations send out radio programmes for you to listen to.

The sounds travel through the air as **radio waves** which cannot be seen, felt or heard.

These waves are picked up by our radio receivers.

They are changed back into sounds and we can listen to the music and voices.

Some people, like this policewoman, use two-way radios for their work.

These radios can send sounds and receive them too.

This means people can talk with each other.

TV TIME

Televisions don't need wires to receive programmes.

The television camera at the studio takes moving pictures which are changed into electronic signals.

Microphones collect the sounds and change these too.

The pictures and sounds are matched together at the broadcasting station.

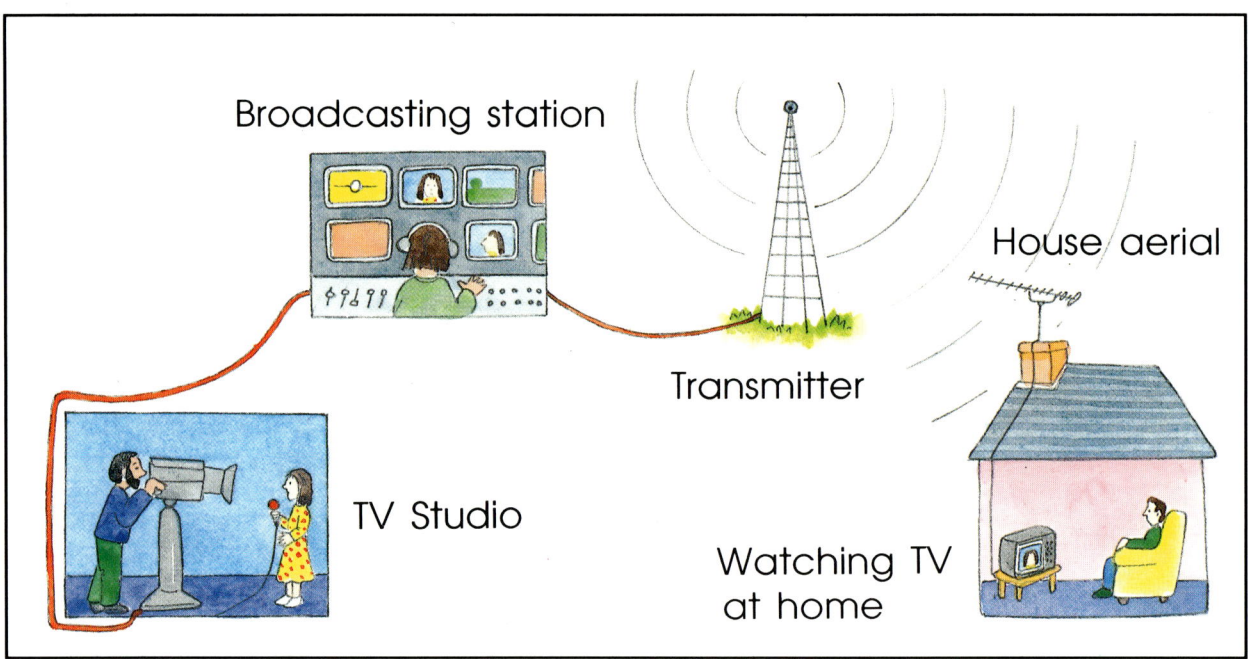

They are sent out through the air in invisible waves. These are picked up by your television **aerial**.

When you switch on your television, it receives the waves and changes them back to pictures and sounds.

The TV show is filmed in the studio.
We can watch it when we are sitting at home.

The band is playing to a small audience. Many more people can hear them if their music is recorded.

PLAY IT AGAIN

Many people like to hear their favourite music played over again.

They can buy **records**, **compact discs** or tapes like these.

Find some to take a close look at.

Tape recorders are useful in offices, schools and homes.

They record on to a special magnetic tape. This changes sounds into electronic signals and stores them.

We can record our own voices, or programmes from the radio, on to the tape.

Learn how to record your voice on a tape recorder.

Work with some friends to record the news from around your school.

MOVING MOMENTS

Video cameras record moving pictures and sounds straight on to a magnetic tape.

The video tape can be played back on a video recorder and shown on a TV set or used in a studio.

We can buy video tapes of films and television programmes to play back on our video recorders.

We can record our favourite programmes on to blank video tapes.

Later, we can watch them as many times as we like.

Video tapes can be used to record lessons.

Some people like to play back their weddings on video.

Sports people can watch their mistakes on tape.

Banks use them to record robberies and catch thieves.

Find out how else video recording can be useful.

People use video cameras to take pictures and sounds. They can record a lovely day and watch it again later.

These people are using **computers** at work.
The computer screens can give lots of information.

GIVING ORDERS

Computers can do many clever things.
They are very quick and save us time, but they cannot think for themselves.

We have to tell them what to do. They need a **program**. We use a keyboard to give orders to a computer.

The keyboard has numbers and letters. We press the keys and the words and symbols appear on a screen.

Ask an adult to help you load the computer with the program you wish to use.

When the computer has read it a flashing light, called a cursor, shows on the screen.

You can move this in all directions.

Find a program that helps you practise using the keyboard.

You can use a program with pictures too.

A GOOD PROGRAM

Computers store information on **silicon chips**.

Silicon chips are tiny. They can be used in watches, hand-held games and calculators.
Each chip has a built-in program like a tiny computer.

Large computers can use many different programs. These are stored on discs or tape. They make the computer take our instructions to do different things.

Work in twos. Ask your teacher for ten sums.

One of you can work them out in your head. The other can use a calculator.

Write down the answers. Which way is quicker?

Ask your teacher to check the answers. Which way is more accurate?

Swap over and do it again with ten more sums, just to make sure your results are right.

The computer game is very exciting.
You have to be quick on the keys to win the game.

PRINT OUT

The printing machine is plugged into the computer. We press keys to tell the computer to make it print. The information we want is printed on to paper.

Some printers have wires which smack against an inky ribbon.

They print a row of dots which are grouped together to form a letter or number.

This is called dot matrix printing.

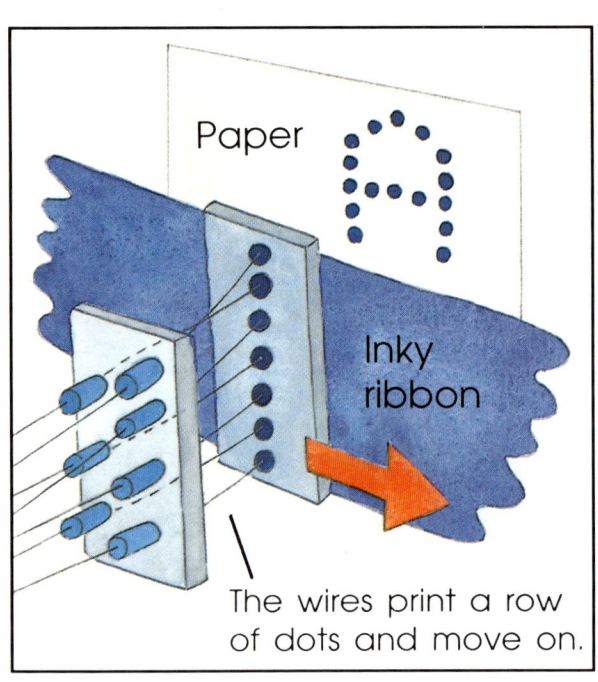

The wires print a row of dots and move on.

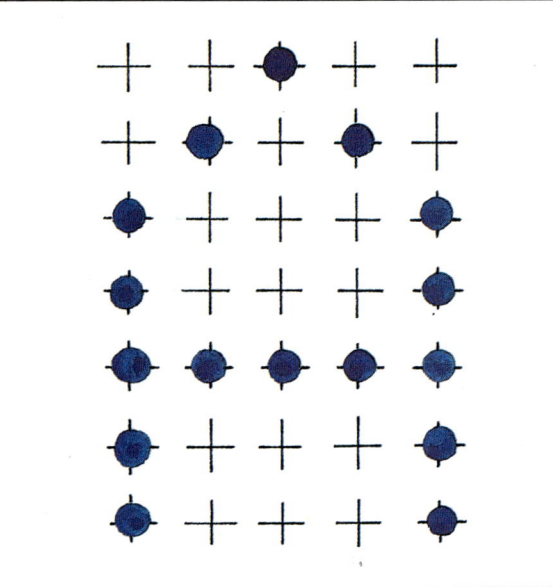

Can you draw some letters using dots?

Try the letter A first. Does it take you long?

Watch how quickly a printing machine works.

Find out about other ways of printing used today.

The machines are told what to print from the computers. They can print each letter quicker than you can see it.

The **laser** light reads the bar codes on the shopping. The supermarket's data bank tells the till what it costs.

SAFE IN THE BANK

A data bank is a store of information in a computer.

Many shops, businesses and libraries use data banks.

The information has to be put into the data bank first and then it can be used again and again.

All sorts of goods and books carry bar codes.

Bar codes are like keys to unlock information in the data bank.

They are patterns of stripes with numbers.

A laser light reads the stripes and turns them into computer language.

The computer can then release information stored in the data bank.

Can you find a bar code on the back of this book?

Satellite dishes point up to the sky.
They receive and send messages to satellites in space.

SATELLITES IN SPACE

Satellites are taken into space by rocket launcher or space shuttle. They are left in orbit around the Earth.

They receive information and pass it back to Earth.

They can tell us what the weather is doing and about the planets in space.

They can send TV programmes and telephone conversations around the world.

Cover a cardboard roll with foil.

Stick oblongs of foil on the ends of two lollipop sticks.

Fit the sticks into slits in the roll.

These will look like solar panels. They give power to the satellites.

GLOSSARY

Aerial Part of a television or radio which receives signals.

Compact disc A small disc on which sound has been recorded using a laser.

Computer A machine which takes in, stores and gives us information.

Fax machine A machine which can send and receive writing and pictures through a telephone line.

Laser A special kind of light.

Optic fibres Lengths of thin glass threads which carry messages in the form of light.

Program A set of instructions for a computer.

Record A disc which has sound recorded on it by cutting grooves into the plastic.

Satellite A machine sent into space to send and receive messages.

Sign language Instead of speaking, hands are used to show letters and words.

Silicon chips Very tiny square shapes that hold information for computers.

Waves Invisible signals sent through the air.

FINDING OUT MORE

Books to read:

Computers by Angela Grunsell (Franklin Watts, 1989)
Lasers by David Jefferis (Franklin Watts, 1989)
Satellites by Angela Grunsell (Franklin Watts, 1989)

Teachers' resource:

Using Computers Effectively (Scholastic, 1989)

PICTURE ACKNOWLEDGEMENTS

Chapel Studios 8, 13, 17 top, 18, 19; David Cumming 7; Tony Stone Worldwide 5, 10, 20, 25, 26, 28; Topham 1, 15; Wayland Picture Library (Zul Mukhida) cover, 17 bottom, 21, 22, 29; Tim Woodcock 4; ZEFA 16, 23.
Artwork illustrations by Rebecca Archer.
The publishers would also like to thank Davigdor Infants' School and Somerhill Road County Primary School, Hove, and St Bernadette's First & Middle School, Brighton, East Sussex, for their kind co-operation.

INDEX

Page numbers in **bold** indicate subjects shown in pictures, but not mentioned in the text on those pages.

Aerial 14, 30

Bar codes 26, 27
Broadcasting station 13, 14

Calculators 22
Compact discs 16, 17, 30
Computers **10**, 20, 21, 22, 23, 24, 25, 27, 30
Cursor 21

Data Bank 26, 27
Discs 16, 17, 22
Dot matrix printing 24

Electronic signals 11, 14, 17

Fax machines 11, 30

Information 20, 22, 24, 27, 29

Keyboard **20**, 21, **23**

Language 6, 7
   computer 27
Laser 26, 27, 30
Letters 21, 24, 25
Letters (posting) 8, 9

Microphones 14, **17**

Numbers 21, 24, 27

Optic fibres 11, 30

Pictures 6, 7, 14, 18, 19, 21
Post-code 8, 9
Printing 11, **21**, 24, 25
Program 21, 22, 30,

Radio 12, 13, 17
Recording 16, 17, 18, 19
Records 16, 17, 30

Satellites 11, 28, 29, 30
Sign language 4, 30
Signs 6, 7
Silicon chips 22, 30
Sounds 13, 14, 17, 18, 19
Symbols 21

Talking 4, 13
Tape recorders 17
Tapes 16, 17, 18, 22
Telephone 10, 11, 29
Television (TV) 6, 14, 15, 18, 29

Video 18, 19

Waves 11, 13, 14, 30
Words 4, 5, 6, 21